Internet links

Throughout this book, we have recommended interesting websites where you can find out more about the Roman Army. To visit the recommended sites, go to the **Usborne Quicklinks Website** at www.usborne-quicklinks.com and type the keywords "Roman army". There you will find links to click on to take you to all the sites. Here are some of the things you can do on the recommended sites:

- Take a virtual reality tour of a Roman army fort.

- Look at an interactive map of the empire.

- Find out more about how different war machines and artilliary worked.

Internet safety

When using the Internet, please make sure you follow these guidelines:

- Ask your parent's or guardian's permission before you connect to the Internet.

- When you are on the Internet, never tell anyone your full name, address or telephone number, and ask an adult before you give your email address.

- If a website asks you to log in or register by typing your name or email address, ask an adult's permission first.

- If you do receive an email from someone you don't know, tell an adult and do not reply to the email.

Computer not essential

If you don't have access to the Internet, don't worry. This book is a complete, superb, self-contained reference book on its own.

Site availability

The links in **Usborne Quicklinks** are regularly reviewed and updated, but occasionally you may get a message that a site is unavailable. This might be temporary, so try again later, or even the next day. If any of the sites close down, we will, if possible, replace them with suitable alternatives, so you will always find an up-to-date list of sites in **Usborne Quicklinks**.

What you need

Most websites listed in this book can be accessed using a standard home computer and a web browser (the software that lets you look at information from the Internet). Some sites need extra programs (plug-ins) to play sound or show videos or animations. If you go to a site and do not have the necessary plug-in, a message will come up on the screen. There is usually a button on the site that you can click on to download the plug-in. Alternatively, go to **Usborne Quicklinks** and click on **Net Help**. There, you can find links to download plug-ins.

Notes for parents and guardians

The websites described in this book are regularly reviewed and the links in **Usborne Quicklinks** are updated. However, the content of a website may change at any time and Usborne Publishing is not responsible for the content on any website other than its own.

We recommend that children are supervised while on the Internet, that they do not use Internet chat rooms, and that you use Internet filtering software to block unsuitable material. Please ensure that your children read and follow the safety guidelines printed on the left. For more information, see the "**Net Help**" area on the **Usborne Quicklinks Website.**

Roman
Army

Ruth Brocklehurst

Designed by Lucy Owen and Stephen Wright

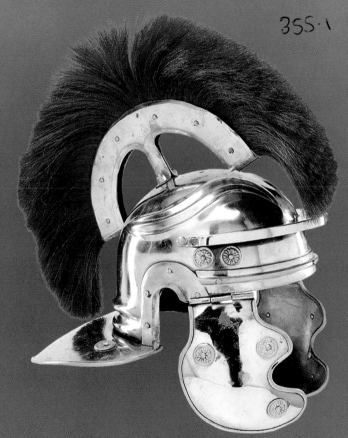

Edited by Jane Chisholm
Illustrated by Inklink, Giacinto Gaudenzi, Ian Jackson and John Woodcock
Consultant: Dr Andrew Gardner
Institute of Archaeology, University College London

Contents

Internet links

Look for the Internet links boxes throughout this book. They contain descriptions of websites where you can find out more about the Roman army. For links to these websites, go to **www.usborne-quicklinks.com** and type in the keywords "roman army".

★ Some of the pictures in the book have a star symbol beside them. It means you can download the pictures from the **Usborne Quicklinks Website**. For more information, and for safety guidelines for using the Internet, and downloading Usborne pictures, see inside the cover.

Dates

Many of the dates in this book are from the time before the birth of Christ. They are shown by the letters BC, which stand for "Before Christ". Dates in this period are counted backwards. Dates after Christ's birth are shown by the letters AD, which stand for *Anno Domini* (Latin for "Year of our Lord").

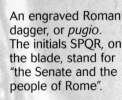

An engraved Roman dagger, or *pugio*. The initials SPQR, on the blade, stand for "the Senate and the people of Rome".

Who were The Romans? ....

The Roman army was the driving force behind one of the greatest empires of the ancient world. It all began around 3,000 years ago when members of a tribe, called the Latins, settled on a group of hills in Italy. Their hilltop villages eventually grew into the magnificent city of Rome. Its people, the Romans, built up a great army and conquered many lands around the Mediterranean Sea. Within 500 years, they had become the world's first superpower.

An expanding empire

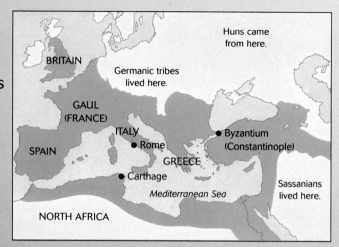

The green parts of this map show the lands of the Roman Empire, at its largest, in AD117.

The Republic of Rome

At first, Rome was ruled by kings. But, in around 510BC, the people drove out their king and elected a group of men from important Roman families to rule them instead. This system of government is called a republic. The Roman Republic was ruled by a group of men called senators. Together they were known as the Senate.

In the early years, the Romans fought many wars to defend their land against invaders. But, as their army grew more powerful, they took land from their enemies. By 264BC, the Romans dominated all of Italy. Then they began to extend their empire by conquering other lands, which they divided into areas called provinces.

The Roman people

People who were born in Rome were known as citizens. This meant they could vote in elections and serve in the army. Life was harder for non-citizens – slaves or people from outside the city – who had few rights. In later years, the Romans gave citizenship to many of the people they conquered.

Temple of Vesta where a sacred fire was kept burning.

The fall of the Republic

The Roman Republic lasted nearly 500 years. But, in around 130BC, while its leaders were fighting to gain territories overseas, things began to fall apart at home. Senators and army generals competed for power and civil war broke out, as they set their armies against each other.

Imperial Rome

A general named Julius Caesar brought peace back to Rome in 45BC. But, the next year, he was killed by his rivals and civil war broke out again. In 27BC, Caesar's heir, Octavian, dissolved the Republic and made himself the sole ruler of Rome. He took the name "Augustus" and became the first of many Roman emperors. The rule of the emperors lasted for another 500 years.

A laurel wreath

This is a reconstruction of the heart of Imperial Rome.

Temple of Jupiter

Painted statues

Temple of the god Saturn

The public records office

Arch of Septimus Severus

The *Curia*, where the Senate met.

Speakers' platform, or *rostra*

Public ceremonies were held in this area.

Shrine to the goddess of the sewer

A soldier and his weapons

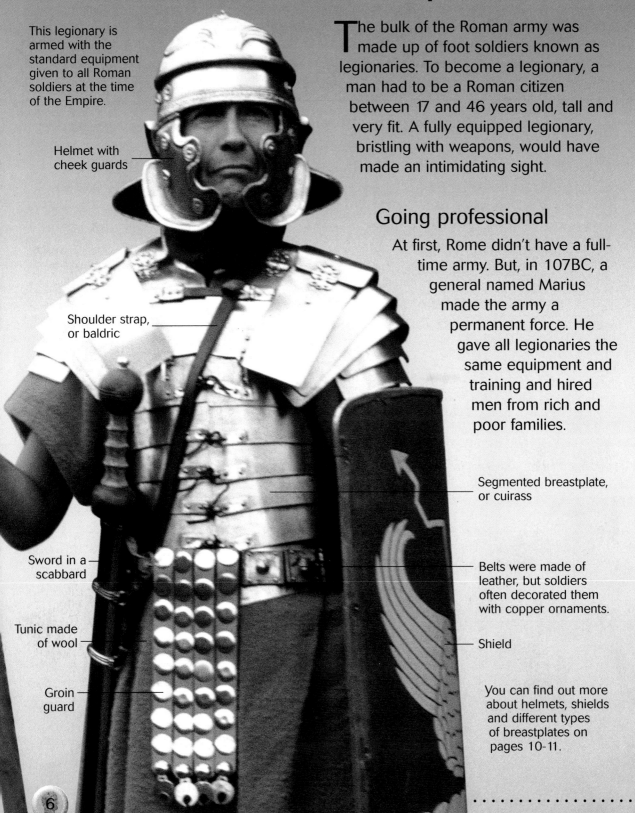

This legionary is armed with the standard equipment given to all Roman soldiers at the time of the Empire.

Helmet with cheek guards

Shoulder strap, or baldric

Sword in a scabbard

Tunic made of wool

Groin guard

The bulk of the Roman army was made up of foot soldiers known as legionaries. To become a legionary, a man had to be a Roman citizen between 17 and 46 years old, tall and very fit. A fully equipped legionary, bristling with weapons, would have made an intimidating sight.

Going professional

At first, Rome didn't have a full-time army. But, in 107BC, a general named Marius made the army a permanent force. He gave all legionaries the same equipment and training and hired men from rich and poor families.

Segmented breastplate, or cuirass

Belts were made of leather, but soldiers often decorated them with copper ornaments.

Shield

You can find out more about helmets, shields and different types of breastplates on pages 10-11.

Javelins

Every legionary was armed with a javelin known as a *pilum*. It was 2m (6.5ft) long with a pointed iron head on a narrow iron neck, fixed to a wooden shaft. When a legionary threw his *pilum* at an enemy fighter, its sharp tip easily penetrated his shield or even his flesh.

The iron part of a *pilum* was almost 1m (3.3ft) long.

This is a sword, or *gladius*. It was 60cm (2ft) long and was kept in a scabbard.

Scabbard

Latin words

Some of the words in this book are written in *italics* to show that they are in Latin, the Romans' language. In Latin, singular nouns ending in *-um* or *-us* change to *-a* or *-i* in the plural. For example one *pilum*, two *pila*, one *gladius*, two *gladii*.

Flashing blades

For close combat, a legionary carried a pointed dagger and a stabbing sword called a *gladius*. A thrusting jab with its deadly double-edged blade could kill an enemy soldier outright.

Belting-up

The sword and dagger were kept in scabbards, hung from a belt the legionary wore around his waist or from a shoulder strap called a baldric. A groin guard made of studded leather strips also hung from the belt. This gave protection, but also made a fearsome jangling noise as legionaries charged at the enemy.

A legionary always wore his dagger on the left-hand side.

Fact: Legionaries were among the best-paid Roman workers. They usually earned about twice what most farm workers made, all paid in silver coins called *denarii*.

Organizing the army

The Roman army was a massive military force. It was also the most disciplined and well-organized army of ancient times. The army was divided into large fighting units called legions. The size of the army varied over the years, but at its peak, under Augustus, there were 28 legions (about 140,000 men).

The soldiers

The Roman army employed many different types of soldiers at various levels of importance, or rank. The main soldiers are shown on this page.

A legate was in charge of a legion.

Six tribunes helped each legate to run the legion.

The camp prefect was in charge of building and training.

A general commanded several legions.

The *primus pilus* was the most senior centurion in a legion.

A centurion led a century (see opposite).

A legionary was a citizen foot soldier.

An archer fought with bows and arrows. Archers came from the Middle East, and dressed differently from the Romans.

A cavalry soldier fought on horseback.

A non-citizen fighter was called an auxiliary.

★

An Imperial legion

Under Emperor Augustus, each legion comprised over 5,000 men, organized into small groups in which every man knew his place. The legion was made up of the first cohort, of 800 men, and nine ordinary cohorts of 480 men. Each ordinary cohort contained six centuries of 80 men. A century was divided into 10 *contubernia* of 8 men each.

This diagram shows the groups that made up an Imperial legion.

Nine ordinary cohorts (6 centuries in each)

First cohort, made up of 800 men

6 centuries of 80 men each

10 *contubernia* had 8 soldiers in each.

Internet links

For a link to a website where you can read about the Roman army and play a fun quiz, go to **www.usborne-quicklinks.com**

Centurions wore a crest like this on their helmets so they could be easily spotted by their men.

Fact: At first, a century was made up of 100 soldiers, taking its name from *cent*, the Latin for 100. Later, the number changed but the name stayed the same.

9

Protection

A blow from an enemy fighter's sword could be lethal, so soldiers needed to be well protected. Over his tunic, each legionary wore a metal body suit. To protect his head and neck, he had a sturdy iron or bronze helmet. Each soldier also carried a large, curved shield.

Internet links

For a link to a website where you can find out more about Roman army equipment, go to **www.usborne-quicklinks.com**

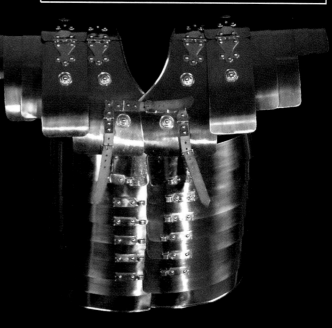

Body protection

Legionaries wore three main kinds of body protection over their tunics. The most common was the segmented breastplate. This was made from overlapping iron and copper bands fixed to leather strips, which allowed the body to move easily. Chain mail and scale mail were also worn by auxiliaries.

Leather laces were tied through the brass fittings down the front of the breastplate to fasten it.

Segmented breastplates were the most effective kind of body protection.

Chain mail shirts were made from thousands of metal rings, linked together.

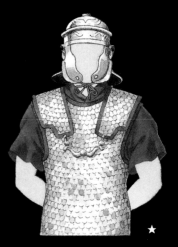

Scale mail was made by sewing tiny metal scales onto a fabric or leather vest.

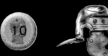

Fact: The legionary shield, or *scutum*, was very heavy. It weighed around 7.5kg (16.5lb) — that's nearly as much as eight packs of sugar.

Helmet

Roman helmets were made from iron or bronze and lined with felt to make them more comfortable. Most soldiers wore the same style of helmet, whatever their rank, and its design changed little over the years.

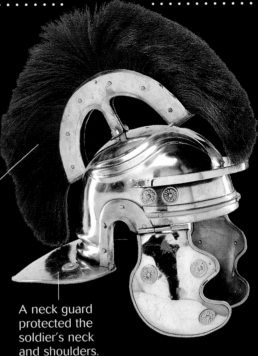

The eyes were shielded by a small peak.

Centurions and their deputies (*optios*) wore a crest on top of their helmets as a sign of authority. This is an *optio*'s helmet.

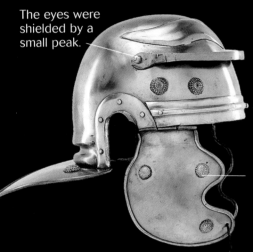

Cheek guards covered the face without obscuring the soldier's vision or hearing.

A neck guard protected the soldier's neck and shoulders.

Shield

Roman soldiers used a large, curved shield called a *scutum*. It was made of plywood covered in leather with a metal disc, or boss, in the middle. The *scutum* wasn't just used for protection. Legionaries also used the shield boss to punch their opponents in the face before stabbing them in the stomach.

Shields were usually red, but varied from one legion to another. The metal boss protected the legionary's hand behind the shield.

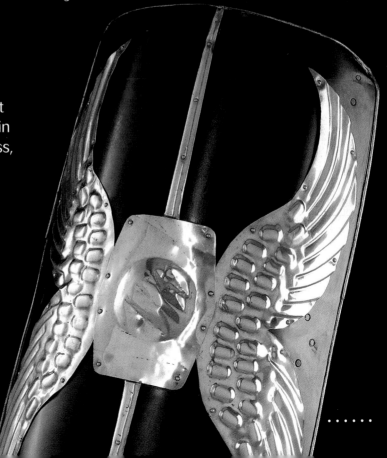

Training and tactics

M ost other armies in the ancient world used similar weapons. But what gave the Roman legionaries the cutting edge was the way they were trained to use their weapons. Roman warfare was not about the skill of the individual. Roman army training made each man as fit and skilled as the next.

Basic training

Before being accepted into the legions, every new recruit had to undergo four months of intensive training. This involved daily drills in weapons-handling, running, jumping and carrying heavy packs. The first thing they were taught was how to march in line and at speed.

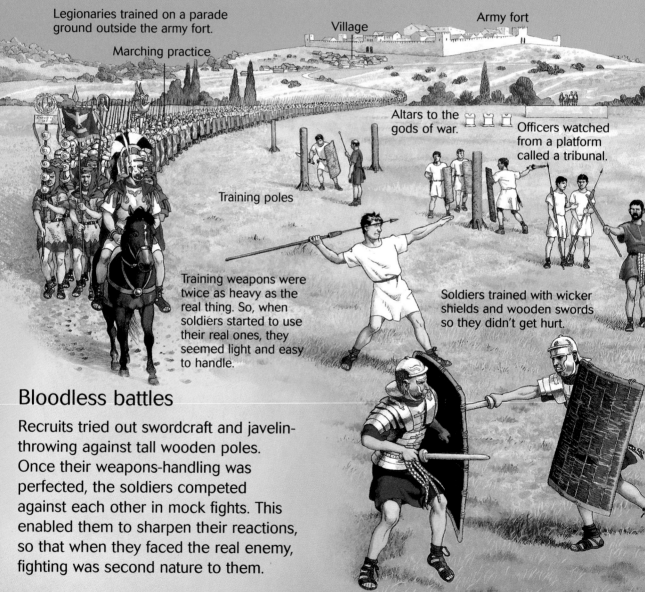

Legionaries trained on a parade ground outside the army fort.

Marching practice

Village

Army fort

Altars to the gods of war.

Officers watched from a platform called a tribunal.

Training poles

Training weapons were twice as heavy as the real thing. So, when soldiers started to use their real ones, they seemed light and easy to handle.

Soldiers trained with wicker shields and wooden swords so they didn't get hurt.

Bloodless battles

Recruits tried out swordcraft and javelin-throwing against tall wooden poles. Once their weapons-handling was perfected, the soldiers competed against each other in mock fights. This enabled them to sharpen their reactions, so that when they faced the real enemy, fighting was second nature to them.

Using the javelin

As a battle opened, legionaries put their training into use as they hurled their javelins, or *pila*, at the enemy. This attack was used to stop the enemy from advancing and to break their ranks.

Internet links

For a link to a website where you can read all about the day in the life of a legionary, including his training drills, go to **www.usborne-quicklinks.com**

Once the enemy came within reach, the legions aimed a shower of *pila* at them.

When a *pilum* became lodged in an opponent's shield, he was forced to throw them both away.

Pila were designed to buckle if they hit the ground so the enemy couldn't reuse them.

The legionary jab

The usual way to use a sword is with a wide, swinging action, but the Romans thrust theirs forward with a powerful jab, which was better suited to close combat.

These mock fights were known as *armatura*.

A jab was more accurate than a swing and allowed the legionary to stay safe behind his shield.

Using a wide, swinging action, an enemy soldier exposed himself to the legionary's sword.

Fact: Soldiers trained three times a month to march at a pace of 100 strides a minute. This meant they could cover about 32km (20 miles) in five hours.

War at sea ....

While Rome was gaining control of Italy, the North African city of Carthage was building up an empire of its own. In 264BC, a series of wars, known as the Punic Wars, broke out between the two empires. This gave the Romans their first taste of war at sea and won them their first major conquests overseas. By the time they had won the Punic Wars, the legions had become almost unbeatable.

Rowing and ramming

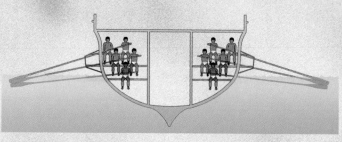

This cross-section of a Roman warship, called a *quinquereme*, shows how sets of five oarsmen were arranged on three levels. ★

Building a fleet

The Carthaginians were experienced sailors, who acquired their wealth by trading goods around the Mediterranean. To defeat the Carthaginians, the Romans would have to face their powerful navy, but they didn't have a fleet of their own. Then they found a wrecked Carthaginian ship and made 120 copies of it.

The battleships of the day were called galleys. They were rowed by oarsmen, arranged on two or three levels. The main tactic was to batter holes in enemy ships with a large ram that stuck out of the front of the ship, just below the water. The crew had to be very skilled to turn and aim the ship quickly and accurately, and to ram as hard as possible.

This scene shows the battle of Actium, between Mark Anthony and Octavian, in 31BC. (See opposite page.)

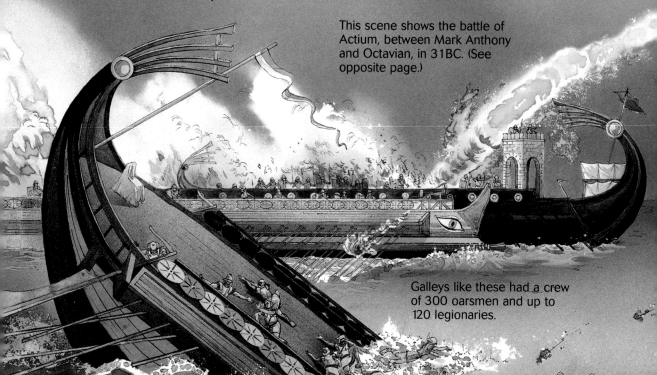

Galleys like these had a crew of 300 oarsmen and up to 120 legionaries.

The cunning crow

Until they invented something called the *corvus* or "crow", the Romans were poor seamen. This was a spiked drawbridge, which dropped down from a Roman galley onto an enemy ship. This allowed legionaries to charge aboard to fight the Carthaginians hand-to-hand – so sea battles became land battles. This helped the Romans to smash the Carthaginian navy and claim Sicily as their first province.

The *corvus* swivelled around a pole on the deck of the galley. This meant it could be dropped onto a ship on either side of it.

The spike on the *corvus* crashed into the deck of the Carthaginian ship, locking the two boats together as the Romans charged across.

The navy and the Empire

After the Punic Wars, the Romans ruled the sea and their navy protected their trade ships. The only major sea battle after that was between Octavian and his rival, Mark Anthony, as they fought for control of the empire.

Internet links

For a link to a website where you can find out more about Roman ships, go to **www.usborne-quicklinks.com**

The ships had huge catapults to fire rocks and flaming missiles at their opponents.

Towers on the decks enabled archers to aim down at soldiers on the decks of enemy ships.

Hannibal

L osing a war to the Romans involved giving up territory and paying huge fines. The First Punic War left the Carthaginians broke and without an empire. But, they began to build a new one in Spain. In 218BC, they invaded Italy and war broke out again. The Second Punic War was one of the most famous and hard-fought wars in Roman history.

Over the Alps

Marching through the steep, narrow passes of the Alps was the final test of endurance. It was winter and bitterly cold. Many died of hunger or lost their footing on the ice, plummeting to their deaths. Hannibal lost half his army and most of his elephants.

Hannibal on the warpath

A great Carthaginian general named Hannibal set out from southern Spain to invade Italy. As the Romans controlled the sea, he decided to surprise them by marching across land. It was a journey of epic proportions, with 60,000 men and around 40 war elephants. It took three months just to get across the Pyrenees mountains, with little food and battling against hostile local tribes on the way.

Internet links

For a link to a website where you can find out more about Hannibal and the people of Carthage, go to **www.usborne-quicklinks.com**

This map shows the lands ruled by Rome by the end of the Punic Wars.

ALPS

ITALY

PYRENEES

CORSICA

Rome

Cannae

SPAIN

SARDINIA

Capua

MEDITERRANEAN SEA

SICILY

Carthage

Zama

☐ Roman lands before the Punic Wars

➚ Hannibal's route 2,420km (1,500miles)

☐ Carthaginian lands taken by Rome after the Punic Wars

First Punic War, 264-41BC After a number of battles, on sea and land, Rome took Sicily, conquering Sardinia and Corsica later.

Second Punic War, 218-202 Battle of Cannae, 218AD Hannibal's army killed around 50,000 Romans and captured 14,000. **Battle of Zama, 202BC** The Romans defeated the Carthaginians and seized their territories in Spain and North Africa.

Third Punic war, 149-146 The Romans conquered the Carthaginians and destroyed their city for good.

Hannibal leads his army over the Alps. Historians believe he used African forest elephants, which are now endangered.

Hannibal and Scipio

The Romans heard of Hannibal's plans and sent their army to northern Italy to confront him. They thought Hannibal's ragged army would be no match for the legions. But Hannibal's superior tactics won him battle after battle. He wreaked havoc, occupying much of Italy for 16 years. Unable to defeat him in Italy, a Roman general named Scipio attacked Carthage. Hannibal went back to defend it, but was finally defeated at Zama.

Outwitting the elephants

Hannibal had 80 elephants in his front line at Zama. But, as they charged at the Romans, Scipio ordered his army to step aside. The elephants charged straight through the gaps, leaving the legions free to deal with the Carthaginians.

Once the elephants started their charge, it was difficult to make them stop and turn around.

★

Fact: Hannibal built huge rafts to get across the Rhône river. The rafts were covered in turf so the elephants would think they were still on dry land.

Army on the march

With a vast empire to defend, and wars to fight in its most distant corners, the Roman army had a lot of ground to cover. Legionaries were trained to march long distances and set up camp quickly and efficiently. This meant they didn't lay themselves open to attack in hostile territory.

Marching orders

Roman soldiers usually marched in a column, six men wide. The column was organized in legions that could react swiftly to attacks. Auxiliary soldiers marched ahead of the army to ward off the enemy. They were followed by surveyors and engineers, who marked out the campsite and cleared the land. By the time the legions at the back arrived, the camp was already built.

Legionaries on the march carried weapons, food, cooking pots and digging tools on poles over their shoulders.

The Roman army usually camped on high ground so that they could see enemies approaching from miles around.

The dirt from the ditch was piled into a mound and stakes were driven into it to make a rampart.

Legionaries' tent

Centurion's tent

Soldiers guarded the entrance to the camp at all times.

A ditch and rampart made it difficult for the enemy to invade the camp.

Internet links

For a link to a website where you can see videos of the Roman army on campaign, go to **www.usborne-quicklinks.com**

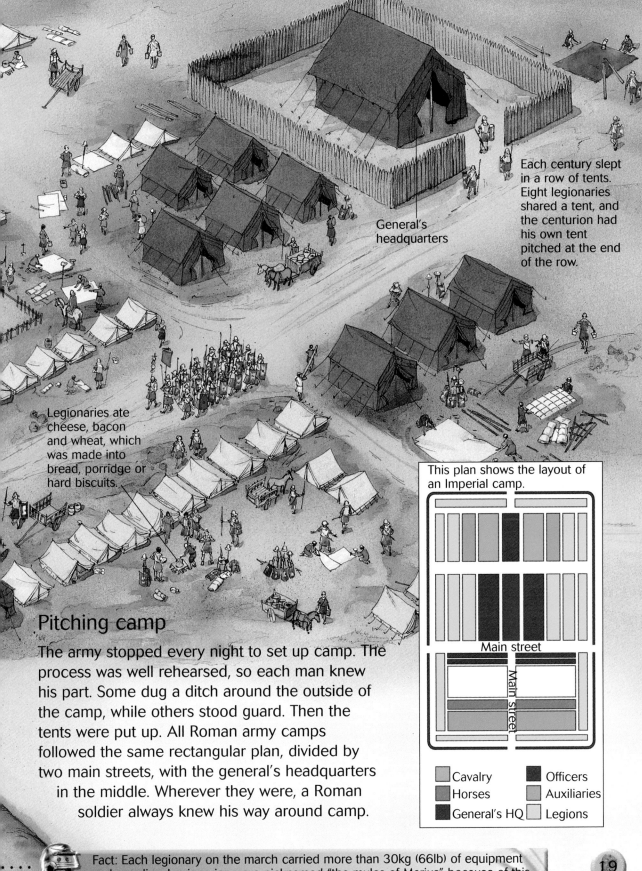

General's headquarters

Each century slept in a row of tents. Eight legionaries shared a tent, and the centurion had his own tent pitched at the end of the row.

Legionaries ate cheese, bacon and wheat, which was made into bread, porridge or hard biscuits.

This plan shows the layout of an Imperial camp.

Main street

Main street

Cavalry	Officers
Horses	Auxiliaries
General's HQ	Legions

Pitching camp

The army stopped every night to set up camp. The process was well rehearsed, so each man knew his part. Some dug a ditch around the outside of the camp, while others stood guard. Then the tents were put up. All Roman army camps followed the same rectangular plan, divided by two main streets, with the general's headquarters in the middle. Wherever they were, a Roman soldier always knew his way around camp.

Fact: Each legionary on the march carried more than 30kg (66lb) of equipment and supplies. Legionaries were nicknamed "the mules of Marius" because of this.

The standards

Roman military standards stood for the prestige and glory of Rome and were proudly guarded. They were carried on tall poles ahead of the army in battle. The Romans valued them so highly that sometimes they even fought wars to recover standards that had been seized by enemy troops.

Emperors and eagles

Each legion had two main standards. One showed a portrait of the emperor, to remind the men of their loyalty to him. The other was an eagle, made from silver or gold, with thunderbolts held between its claws. The eagle standard, or *aquifer*, was the symbol of the whole army.

The gilt portrait of the emperor was known as the *imago*.

The thunderbolts represent Jupiter, king of the Roman gods.

Name and number

When a group of soldiers went ahead of their legion, they carried a banner called a *vexillum*. This showed the legion's emblem, its name and number. The emblem was usually a sign of the zodiac.

Each century also had its own standard, called a *signum*. This was a long pole decorated with medals and the unit's emblems. In the battlefield, soldiers could easily spot their *signum* and follow it.

Vexillum

Signum

Standard bearers wore animal skins on their helmets to make them look ferocious.

This extraordinary trumpet called a *cornu* would have sounded loudly over the legionaries' heads to convey orders to them.

Fact: Only the most trustworthy soldiers could become standard bearers because it was also their job to look after the soldiers' pay and savings.

Battle plans

Full-scale battles were usually fought between armies of thousands. This meant heavy losses on both sides, so the Romans never went into battle unless they were sure they could win. To ensure a victory, generals always gave their troops a good night's rest, a slap-up meal and a motivating speech. They also had various strategies which could be adapted to any conditions.

1 century (80 men) Front line of legionaries

1 century (80 men) Second line of legionaries

Roman cavalry

Enemy troops

Direction of attack

These diagrams show some of the Roman army's most successful battle strategies.

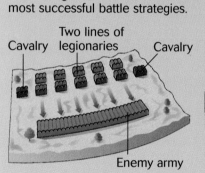

Cavalry Two lines of legionaries Cavalry

Enemy army

1. At the order, the front line of legionaries charged forward.

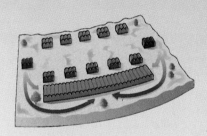

2. The cavalry rode around their opponents to attack their weak spots, at the sides and at the back, and to surround them.

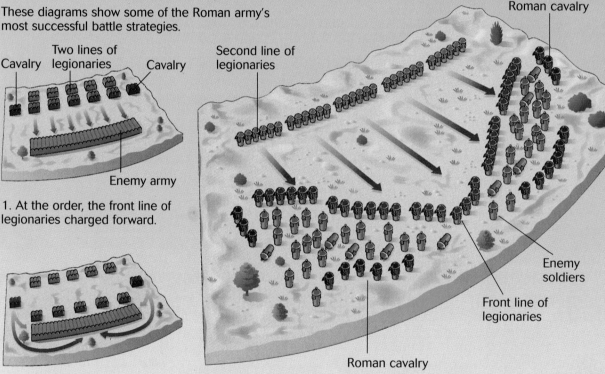

Roman cavalry

Second line of legionaries

Enemy soldiers

Front line of legionaries

Roman cavalry

3. The second line of legionaries was held in reserve. They moved forward to replace tired or injured soldiers. Once the Romans had broken up the enemy's front line, it was usually just a matter of time before the enemy was beaten.

The lie of the land

The Romans chose their battlegrounds carefully, to give themselves the advantage over their opponents. Ideally, they took the higher ground, with the sun and wind behind them. This gave them the best view of the battlefield, while the enemy was blinded by the sun and dust. The best ground was flat and open, where the enemy had no place to hide.

Battle formations

The Romans had different formations for particular situations. These included the "orb" to defend themselves, and the "wedge" to attack. The most famous Roman battle formation was the "tortoise" or *testudo* – the Roman equivalent of a tank.

The soldiers formed the "orb" when they were surrounded by the enemy. Legionaries formed the outer circle, while archers and officers stood inside.

Legionaries preparing to throw their *pila*

The "wedge" was a v-shaped formation, with one man at the front tip. It was used to break up and push back the opponent's front line.

If legionaries were ambushed by enemy cavalry, they made their shields and *pila* into a spiked wall to stop the horses in their tracks. The men at the back threw their *pila* at the enemy.

The overlapped shields of the *testudo* made a missile-proof shell as legionaries advanced on enemy ground.

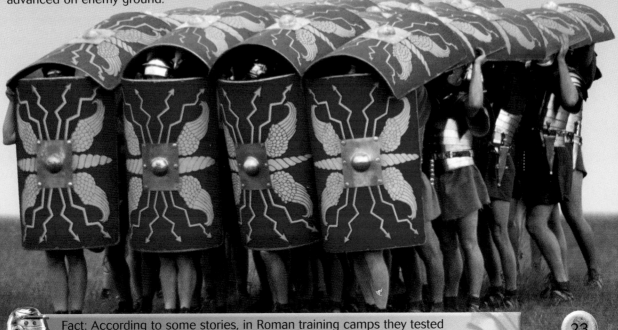

Fact: According to some stories, in Roman training camps they tested the strength of the *testudo* by driving a cart over the top of it.

23

An army life

A soldier's rank in the army depended as much on his family background as on his ability. Although a common citizen could work his way up through the ranks, officers were usually recruited from the upper classes. Whatever his class, an army life offered a man the chance to move up in the world.

Career climbing

A legionary began his army career as a lowly *miles*, doing all the dirty jobs. If he worked and fought hard, he would be promoted to *immunis*. This meant he could specialize in a trade.

The duties of a *miles* included cleaning the army's latrines.

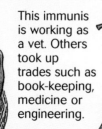

This immunis is working as a vet. Others took up trades such as book-keeping, medicine or engineering.

The army oath

When a man joined the army, he swore allegiance to Rome, promising to fight to the death. From then on, he belonged to the army.

The whole army renewed their vow every new year.

Crime and punishment

Roman army discipline was strict and swift. If a man misbehaved, he would be punished severely. Punishment ranged from beatings or demotion, to fines or even execution. The threat of punishment alone was usually enough to keep soldiers in line.

Centurions were responsible for discipline. They used a stick to beat disobedient soldiers.

Fact: The most brutal punishment was the execution of every tenth man in a mutinous cohort. This was called decimation, from *decem*, the Latin for "ten".

Moving up

If a legionary proved to be brave and loyal, the next step up was to become a *principale* or a centurion. The highest-ranking centurion in a legion was the *primus pilus*. This position meant that his sons could become senators.

When legionaries retired, many built large houses, called villas, like the ones in this Roman fresco.

The *principales* included standard bearers.

The *primus pilus* commanded the first century of the first cohort.

Retirement

After 20-26 years with the army, a legionary was given a pension or a plot of land to live on. Auxiliaries and their families were granted Roman citizenship. This promised a better life for their sons, who could join the legions.

The Emperor was the head of the army. The word "emperor" comes from the Latin, *Imperator*, which means "general".

One tribune in each legion was a young senator. He had a purple stripe on his tunic to show his status.

Officers

Young aristocrats joined the army as tribunes or as junior officers in charge of auxiliary units. Some went up through the ranks to become generals. Others only served for around four years, in training for a political career.

Construction work

Many Roman soldiers were not just highly trained fighters; they were also skilled builders, engineers, stone masons or carpenters. These skills were essential for setting up camps and building forts. But they were also useful for other building work during peacetime.

Roadworks

This cross-section of a Roman road shows how they were built.

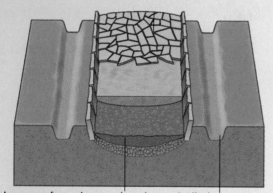

Layers of sand, gravel and rocks were packed into a trench under a hard-wearing surface of stone slabs.

A ditch on either side of the road drained water away.

★

The army built up a vast network of roads so they could reach every corner of the empire as quickly as possible. The roads were designed to follow the straightest, flattest route and were built to last. Many roads in Europe today still follow the routes taken by the Romans.

On the road

Roman roads played an important part in the running of the empire. Horseback messengers used the roads to deliver official news to and from the emperor. If trouble was reported in the provinces, soldiers could march straight there to sort it out. The roads also helped trade between different parts of the empire.

Internet links

For a link to a website with diagrams, maps and photographs of Roman roads, go to
www.usborne-quicklinks.com

Building bridges

When the legions reached a large river, they simply built a bridge over it. If they were in a hurry to get across, they lashed boats together to form a temporary bridge. A makeshift wooden road was then placed over the boats, so the army could march across.

Waterways

Another of the army's duties was to construct complex water systems. These systems involved a series of pipes and aqueducts that allowed water to flow downhill, from mountain springs into towns. The water was then piped to toilets, public baths and fountains.

This Roman aqueduct still stands today, near the city of Nîmes, in France.

This picture shows Roman soldiers and engineers building a permanent stone bridge, using a boat bridge, wooden scaffolding and cranes.

Siege tactics ··············

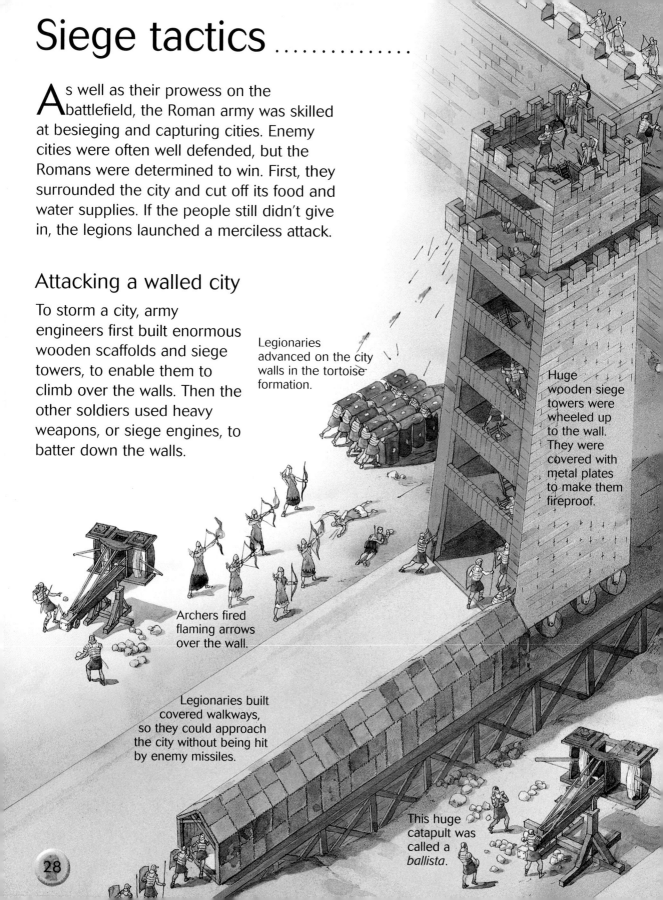

As well as their prowess on the battlefield, the Roman army was skilled at besieging and capturing cities. Enemy cities were often well defended, but the Romans were determined to win. First, they surrounded the city and cut off its food and water supplies. If the people still didn't give in, the legions launched a merciless attack.

Attacking a walled city

To storm a city, army engineers first built enormous wooden scaffolds and siege towers, to enable them to climb over the walls. Then the other soldiers used heavy weapons, or siege engines, to batter down the walls.

Legionaries advanced on the city walls in the tortoise formation.

Huge wooden siege towers were wheeled up to the wall. They were covered with metal plates to make them fireproof.

Archers fired flaming arrows over the wall.

Legionaries built covered walkways, so they could approach the city without being hit by enemy missiles.

This huge catapult was called a *ballista*.

A drawbridge was lowered from the siege tower so the soldiers could invade the city.

Taking captives

Anybody captured during a siege was either killed or sold to wealthy Romans as slaves. Enemy leaders were often executed in public, as a warning to others who tried to resist Roman power.

Soldiers built a ramp over rough ground.

Battering rams were used to smash holes in the walls.

Fact: The Romans used so much timber during the siege of Jerusalem, in AD70, that there were no trees left within 18km (11 miles) of the city.

War machines

Although guns and cannons hadn't been invented, the Romans built powerful weapons, or siege engines, using the latest technology available to them. These machines were designed to cause maximum damage to their enemies' buildings and forts.

The kicking mule

The biggest and most powerful Roman siege engine was called an *onager*. It was a huge one-armed catapult that fired massive missiles. The *onager* took its name from the Latin for "mule" because of the way mules kick rocks behind them.

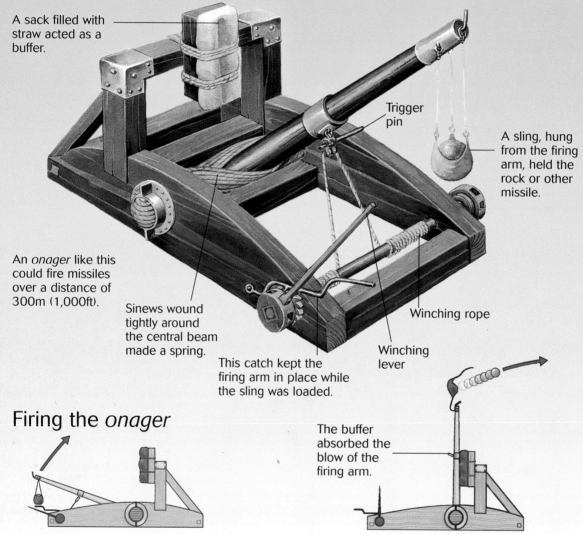

A sack filled with straw acted as a buffer.

Trigger pin

A sling, hung from the firing arm, held the rock or other missile.

An *onager* like this could fire missiles over a distance of 300m (1,000ft).

Sinews wound tightly around the central beam made a spring.

Winching rope

This catch kept the firing arm in place while the sling was loaded.

Winching lever

Firing the *onager*

The buffer absorbed the blow of the firing arm.

The firing arm was hooked to a winching rope, using the trigger pin. Up to four soldiers used the winching lever to wind the arm down. Then, a catch held it down while the sling was loaded.

Next, a soldier knocked out the trigger pin to release the firing arm. The central spring unwound, making the arm shoot forward. When the firing arm hit the buffer, the missile was sent into the air.

Fact: *Onagers* could be loaded with rocks that weighed as much as a grown man. Other missiles the Romans used included red-hot lumps of iron and flaming rags.

Demolition jobs

A battering ram was made from a tree trunk, with a hardened iron tip. It was used to pound at a city's fortifications until the Romans smashed their way in. It was mounted on a wooden frame on wheels and covered with animal skins to protect the soldiers by making a flame-proof shield against enemy missiles.

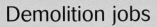

Internet links

For a link to a website where you can find out more about ballistas and other Roman war machines, go to **www.usborne-quicklinks.com**

Giant catapults

Ballistas were large catapults, used to fire arrows and iron-tipped bolts at city walls and enemy soldiers. *Ballistas* varied in size from one man catapults, known as "scorpions" to giant machines that needed as many as ten legionaries to operate them.

This medium-sized *ballista* is being operated by four men.

Defending the borders

In AD 117, Emperor Hadrian inherited an empire that was bigger than it had ever been. He spent a lot of time in the provinces and decided the empire had grown too big to run efficiently. So, he gave up lands in the Middle East. After that, the army's job was to strengthen and defend existing territories, and rarely to conquer more.

Hadrian draws the line

The Romans had never given their empire official borders, because they assumed it would just keep growing. But Hadrian decided to fix the frontiers. So, he posted most of his soldiers in forts along the empire's new borders, so they could defend it from the tribes beyond.

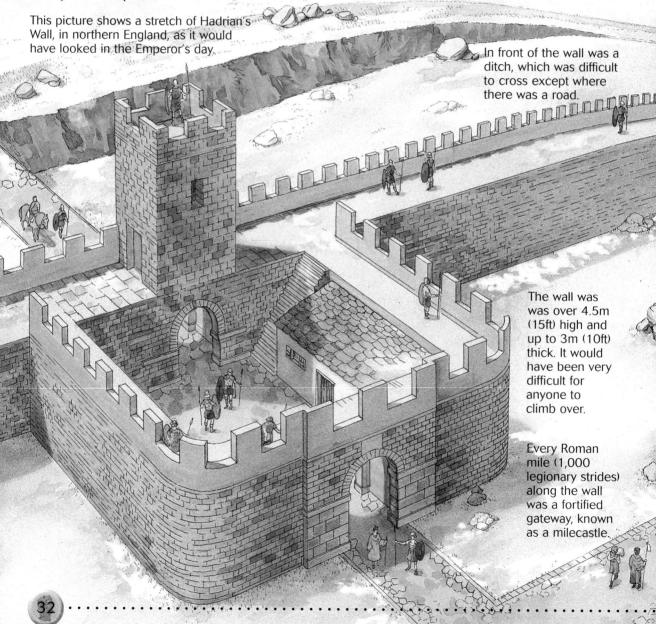

This picture shows a stretch of Hadrian's Wall, in northern England, as it would have looked in the Emperor's day.

In front of the wall was a ditch, which was difficult to cross except where there was a road.

The wall was was over 4.5m (15ft) high and up to 3m (10ft) thick. It would have been very difficult for anyone to climb over.

Every Roman mile (1,000 legionary strides) along the wall was a fortified gateway, known as a milecastle.

Keeping out the rabble

The Romans called the people who lived outside the empire "barbarians" because they thought them wild, aggressive and uncivilized. In Germany, Africa and Britain, they built huge walls and frontier fortifications to stop barbarians from invading, and to control any traffic crossing the borders.

Lookout turrets were built every 500m (1,600ft) along the wall, so soldiers could watch for trouble-makers and pass messages along the wall.

Sixteen auxiliary army forts were built at equal distances from each other along the wall.

Stoneworks

The most impressive frontier fortification anywhere in the empire was Hadrian's Wall. This imposing structure ran for 118km (73 miles) across northern England. The wall wasn't just a solid barrier, but an intimidating reminder, to the local people, of who was in charge.

Internet links

For a link to a website where you can find out about life in a fort on Hadrian's Wall and how the local people really lived outside the Roman empire, go to **www.usborne-quicklinks.com**

A road behind the wall linked the forts together.

A ditch, flanked by mounds gave extra protection south of the wall.

The soldiers controlled local trade by checking who and what crossed the border.

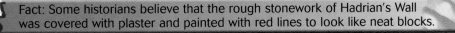

Fact: Some historians believe that the rough stonework of Hadrian's Wall was covered with plaster and painted with red lines to look like neat blocks.

33

Life on the edge ....

By the 2nd century AD, most of the Roman army was posted in forts around the edges of the empire. Soldiers had to keep up the daily training so they were ready for war. But, their main tasks were to enforce the emperor's rule and defend against invasion.

A fort

Roman forts were built in the same way as army camps, but with permanent fortifications. They housed between 800 men and a whole legion and had shrines, bakeries, workshops and hospitals.

Daily routine

Life in a fort was strictly regimented. Soldiers were woken at sunrise and summoned to rollcall by a trumpet blast. At rollcall, they were read a list of duties. After that, they set about training or carrying out their tasks for the day. These included building, farming, guard duty and police work.

This scene shows part of a market town that has grown outside a Roman fort.

New towns

Wherever the army was based, they built roads and aqueducts to bring in all the supplies and fresh water they needed. These improvements attracted local people to settle nearby. Traders saw the soldiers as new customers and set up their stalls outside the fortress gates. Soon, a new town, grew up around the fort.

Soldiers weren't allowed to marry, but many had girlfriends in the town, who they married when they retired.

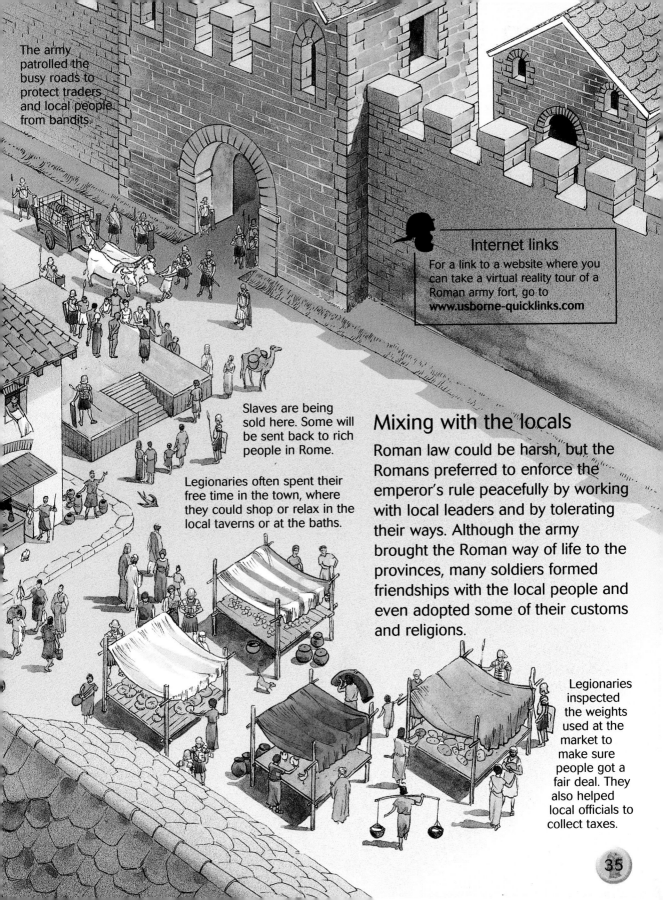

The army patrolled the busy roads to protect traders and local people from bandits.

Internet links

For a link to a website where you can take a virtual reality tour of a Roman army fort, go to www.usborne-quicklinks.com

Slaves are being sold here. Some will be sent back to rich people in Rome.

Legionaries often spent their free time in the town, where they could shop or relax in the local taverns or at the baths.

Mixing with the locals

Roman law could be harsh, but the Romans preferred to enforce the emperor's rule peacefully by working with local leaders and by tolerating their ways. Although the army brought the Roman way of life to the provinces, many soldiers formed friendships with the local people and even adopted some of their customs and religions.

Legionaries inspected the weights used at the market to make sure people got a fair deal. They also helped local officials to collect taxes.

Off duty

Legionaries, like other Roman citizens, spent much of their free time at the Games, which were almost as violent and bloody as any battle. The Games was the name given to races, circus performances, wild animal shows and gladiator fights held in vast arenas.

Chariot racing

One of the most popular public games was chariot racing. There were four teams – green, blue, red and white – each with its own fiercely loyal supporters. There were no rules, so the drivers played dirty. They crashed into each other to knock their rivals off the track. Racers were often thrown from their chariots and trampled to death.

Plays and pantomimes

This mosaic shows two typical theatrical masks of the time – an innocent girl and an evil old man.

The Romans also enjoyed theatrical shows. The most popular were comic tales with music, dancing and special effects. They were usually about familiar types of characters and the actors wore masks to show who they were playing.

A chariot race in Rome's *Circus Maximus*, which held up to 250,000 spectators.

Gladiators

Gladiators were slaves or criminals who were trained to fight each other or even against wild beasts, often to the death. Often the animals were starved and taunted, so they went into a fight hungry and angry. These spectacularly gory fights attracted huge audiences, who were often asked to decide whether the loser should live or die.

This Roman mosaic shows a gladiator fighting a leopard.

Country pursuits

Many soldiers who were rich enough to own horses enjoyed hunting in their free time. They hunted different animals, depending on where in the empire they were based. In the northern provinces, they hunted wild boar and deer. In Africa, they caught leopards, lions and elephants to send back to Rome for the public games.

Dolphin-shaped counters were flipped to mark the end of each lap.

This Egyptian monument, called an obelisk, was brought to Rome by the Emperor Augustus.

Drivers and their horses wore green, blue, red or white to show which team they were racing for.

Chariots were light and built for speed.

Celebrating victory . . . .

Roman senators and emperors realized how easily a dissatisfied army could turn against them. So, legionaries were given regular pay and plenty of rewards for heroic victories, to keep up their loyalty and enthusiasm.

This scene shows a victory parade known as a triumph, through the streets of Rome.

Romans wore their finest clothes and lined the streets to enjoy the triumph.

The general was followed on horseback by his sons and the senior army officers.

A slave held a crown above the general's head, repeating the phrase "remember, you are only a man".

A triumph

If a general gained new territory for the empire, he and his army were rewarded with a festival, known as a triumph. This involved a grand procession through the streets of Rome, followed by feasts, games and shows. The festivities went on all day and long into the night. In later years, triumphs were only awarded to the emperors themselves.

The triumphant general rode in a gilded chariot drawn by four horses. He wore a purple robe and held a laurel branch.

Trumpeters played a fanfare.

Fact: Triumphs usually lasted a day, but the triumph of Flaminius went on for three days, because he and his troops had so much loot to show off.

Crowning glory

Particularly heroic feats were rewarded with crowns, or *corona*. Different crowns were awarded for different achievements, though most were only given to soldiers of higher rank. The most prestigious was the siege crown, given to an officer who set free an army that had been besieged.

The siege crown was made out of woven grasses.

The gold mural crown was given to the first officer over the wall of a besieged city.

Pay and bonuses

Roman soldiers were paid three times a year. But, in addition to their regular pay, legionaries were given bonuses after a victory, and even when a new emperor began his reign. Sometimes they were given a day off to celebrate pay day with sports and games.

An officer who captured an enemy ship was awarded a gold naval crown.

A civic crown of oak leaves, was awarded to a soldier, of any rank, who saved the life of a fellow citizen.

Internet links

For a link to a website where you can spend a day in ancient Rome, go to **www.usborne-quicklinks.com**

Legionaries wore laurel wreaths and chanted victorious songs.

The senators were followed by captured enemy leaders, other prisoners and any riches the Romans had seized from them.

These white oxen were to be sacrificed in the temple of Jupiter after the parade.

Senators marched at the front of the procession.

Anarchy and barbarians

With such a vast empire to govern and defend, no emperor could rule successfully without the help of a loyal army. But, by around AD200, corrupt, ambitious soldiers began to abuse their influence by choosing their own emperors. The empire was weakened by frequent civil wars and attacks from tribes outside. It was the beginning of the end for ancient Rome.

The Anarchy

For fifty years, between 235 and 285, the empire fell into chaos. More than 20 emperors ruled for a short time each, before being deposed or killed by rival army groups. Life was tough for many people, who suffered from rising taxes, as war, plague and famine swept across the empire. Many politicians and army officers tried to seize power in the provinces for themselves. This time of unrest became known as the "Anarchy".

This scene shows a battle between the Roman cavalry and Sassanian horsemen.

Internet links

For a link to a website where you can find out more about the Byzantine empire and its art, go to **www.usborne-quicklinks.com**

Under attack

During the Anarchy, the empire's borders were neglected. Germanic barbarian tribes invaded from the north (see the map on page 4). At the same time, a people called the Sassanians from the Middle East launched massive assaults from the south.

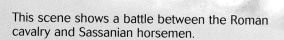
Fact: In 260, the Sassanians managed to capture and kill the Roman emperor, Valerian. Then, they stuffed his body and put it on public display.

The empire splits

In 284, a Roman army general named Diocletian was declared emperor by his army. He realized that the empire had become too big to rule effectively. So he divided it in two. Each half was ruled by an emperor, known as the "Augustus", and his deputy, the "Caesar". Diocletian governed the eastern empire, while another army general, Maximian, ruled in the west.

This statue represents the four rulers of the empire. This system of leadership was known as the "Tetrarchy".

A new capital

When Diocletian and Maximian retired, there was a scuffle for the thrones. Eventually, Constantine became ruler and reunited the two halves of the empire. In 330, Constantine decided that Rome wasn't central enough to be his capital. So he moved it from Rome to Byzantium (see the map on page 4), which he renamed Constantinople.

This is a reconstruction of Constantinople, as it would have looked in around 500.

Huns invade

In around 370, the Huns, a warlike tribe from Central Asia, invaded eastern Europe. They stormed through the land, pushing Germanic tribes into Roman territory. The Romans let the barbarians stay, as long as their warriors fought with the legions to defend the empire.

Rome falls

But this united front didn't last long. In 395, the empire split permanently in two. The Byzantine Empire flourished in the east and lasted for the next 1,000 years. But barbarians overran the west, ransacking Rome and taking control of the army. In 476, a Germanic general named Odoacer declared himself King of Italy. Although Roman rule was over, many Roman ideas about politics and the army still influence people today.

Living history ....

Although it is almost 2,000 years since the Roman empire reached its peak, it made an enormous and lasting impact. Many Roman roads, bridges, buildings and statues were so well made that they have survived the centuries. Archaeologists have dug up all kinds of things - from helmets and swords to coins and sandals - on the sites of Roman army forts. By studying the things the Romans left behind, and reading their writings, historians can find out a lot about them and their extraordinary army.

The carvings on Trajan's column in Rome describe the Romans' victory over Dacia (Romania) in incredible detail. This part shows standard bearers marching over a boat bridge.

Virtual history

Archaeologists make careful measurements of the things they dig up and the places where they came from. All this data can be difficult even for them to sort and interpret. But now, experts can use computer technology and graphics to transform their findings into amazing virtual reality images. Anything, from a fragment of a pot to a ruined building, can be restored to its former glory, and viewed on a computer screen in 3-D.

Virtual reality models enable us to take a "walk", on-screen, through historical places. This model shows the forum in Rome – a meeting place, with shops and temples – as it would have looked 2,000 years ago.

This is a temple dedicated to the worship of Julius Caesar who was made a god after he died.

Written records

Much of what we know about the Roman army comes from the works of ancient writers, who described battles, tactics and the great leaders. Everyday writings, such as military records and soldiers' letters, have also survived. All these written records help us to form a vivid picture of life in the legions.

Internet links

For a link to a website where you can see photographs of a Roman army re-enactment group, go to **www.usborne-quicklinks.com**

Hundreds of soldiers' letters have been found in the ruins of a fort near Hadrian's Wall. Many, like this one, were written on very thin sheets of wood.

Dressing-up

One of the best ways to discover how heavy a legionary's helmet was, or how an *onager* worked, is to try it for yourself. Experimental archaeologists, historians and re-enactment groups reproduce Roman military equipment and battle drills using the same methods and equipment the Romans used. They work with schools and museums to put on public displays that bring the past to life.

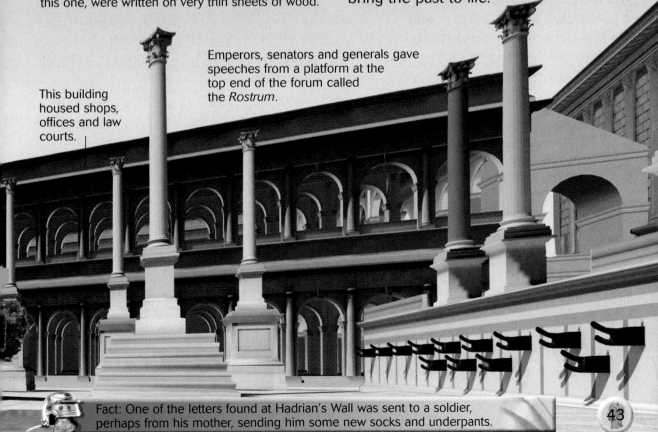

This building housed shops, offices and law courts.

Emperors, senators and generals gave speeches from a platform at the top end of the forum called the *Rostrum*.

Fact: One of the letters found at Hadrian's Wall was sent to a soldier, perhaps from his mother, sending him some new socks and underpants.

Leaders and losers

The names of the greatest Roman leaders, and their deadliest rivals, have become legendary. Here, you can read about some of the most famous characters of the time.

➤ **Hannibal** led the Carthaginians in the Second Punic War. He was defeated by the Romans and spent the rest of his life in exile.

➤ **Fabius** was a consul during the Second Punic War. He saved Rome from the Carthaginians by avoiding direct combat with them. Instead, he and his troops followed Hannibal's army, cutting off their food and water supplies and ambushing smaller units. He was nick-named "the delayer" because of this.

➤ **Marius** was a skilled army general and politician. He is most famous for reforming the Roman army and turning it into a professional force.

➤ **Spartacus** was a slave and gladiator who rebelled against his masters. He raised an army of 90,000 other discontented slaves. His rebel army resisted Roman power for two years. But they were eventually defeated by three Roman legions. Around 6,000 of the slaves were captured and crucified, though Spartacus' body was never found.

➤ **Vercingetorix** was a Gallic chief who led a revolt against the Roman occupation of Gaul. He and his troops were defeated when Julius Caesar launched a relentless siege of the fortified town where they were based.

➤ **Julius Caesar** was probably Rome's greatest general. He conquered Gaul (France) and led his troops to Macedonia and to Britain. In 49BC, Caesar and his army returned to Rome. He defeated his rivals in the senate and declared himself dictator of Rome. But other leaders resented his power and murdered him in 44BC.

This statue shows Julius Caesar in an army general's uniform.

➤ **Augustus**, whose real name was Octavian, was Julius Caesar's heir. He became the first Roman emperor in 31BC after defeating his rivals, Mark Antony and Cleopatra, Queen of Egypt, in the Battle of Actium.

Boudicca was Queen of the Iceni tribe in Britain. In AD60, she led a year-long rebellion against Roman rule. When the Iceni were defeated, Boudicca poisoned herself to avoid the shame of being taken prisoner.

Vespasian was an army general before he became emperor. He strengthened the empire's borders and granted citizenship to many people in the provinces. He began many grand building projects, including the Colosseum in Rome

Josephus was a Jewish general and historian. In AD66, he led a revolt against Roman rule in the province of Judea. When the revolt was crushed, he joined the Romans and wrote a detailed account of their military skill.

Trajan became emperor in AD98. He was one of Rome's most talented military leaders. During his rule, the empire grew to its largest extent.

Marcus Aurelius spent most of his reign, from AD161-180, defending the empire, against barbarian invaders.

Hadrian was a great soldier who became emperor in AD117. He spent much of his rule with his armies and set up permanent fortifications to defend the empire against barbarian invasions.

This imposing bronze statue of Marcus Aurelius was built shortly after his death. It is twice life-size and was originally gilded to look like solid gold.

Diocletian was an army general who was declared emperor by his army in AD284. He divided the Roman empire in two and reformed the army so that its leaders couldn't become too powerful.

Attila, King of the Huns, was one of the most notorious barbarian warriors. He was so bloodthirsty, he is said to have eaten his two sons.

Odoacer was a barbarian general. He sent the last Roman emperor, Augustulus, into exile and declared himself King of Italy in AD476.

Roman army facts

Being a Roman soldier wasn't just about discipline and training. It could also be full of surprise and danger. Here are some of the more fascinating facts about the army and what they did.

➤ The Roman army often kept sacred chickens. Before a battle, Roman generals fed the chickens. If they ate, the gods were on their side. But, it was seen as a bad omen if the chickens refused to eat. On one occasion, when the chickens would not eat, a general called Pulcher threw them into the sea, exclaiming, "If they will not eat, then let them drink!" He lost the battle.

This standard bearer is holding a *vexillum*.

➤ After their victory against the Carthaginians in the Second Punic War, the Romans took the prows, or *rostrata*, of the Carthaginian ships back to Rome as trophies. These were displayed along the front of the speakers' platform in the forum, in Rome which was later named the *rostrum* as a result.

➤ Some legionaries were trained to perform basic surgery on wounded men. It was a painful experience for their patients – the Romans didn't have anaesthetic, and their skills were limited. They were expert at setting broken bones and amputating limbs, but they didn't know how to cure infections or diseases.

➤ Romans were such good engineers that they even designed a ballista that reloaded itself so that it could fire several arrows one after the other. This was the Roman equivalent of a machine gun.

➤ In Roman times, stirrups hadn't been invented and saddles had only recently been introduced. So, staying on the back of a horse in the thick of a battle was quite a skill for a cavalry soldier.

➤ Centurions all carried a stick which they used to beat unruly soldiers. One centurion earned the nickname 'Bring me another' because he beat his men so hard that he was constantly breaking his cane over them and calling for new one.

Index

Acknowledgements ....

Every effort has been made to trace the copyright holders of the material in this book. If any rights have been omitted, the publishers offer to rectify this in any subsequent editions following notification. The publishers are grateful to the following organizations and individuals for their permission to reproduce material (t=top, m=middle, b=bottom, l=left, r=right):

Cover The Ermine Street Guard © National Museums and Galleries of Wales; **p1** Corbis © Archivo Iconografico, S.A./CORBIS; **p2** Corbis © Charles & Josette Lenars/CORBIS; **p6** The Ermine Street Guard © National Museums and Galleries of Wales; **p7** Photographs of weapons by Howard Allman, with special thanks to Arms & Archery, (background) © National Museums and Galleries of Wales; **p10** (background) © Tibor Bognar/CORBIS; **p13** © Charles & Josette Lenars/CORBIS; **p14** © Albion Armourers; **p15** Photographs of helmets and shield by Howard Allman, with special thanks to Arms & Archery; **p20** © Charles & Josette Lenars/CORBIS; **p23** © Charles & Josette Lenars/CORBIS; **p25** © Mimmo Jodice/CORBIS; **p27** © Chris Lisle/CORBIS; **p31** © Charles & Josette Lenars/CORBIS; **p36** © The Art Archive/Museo Capitolino Rome/Dagli Orti; **p37** © Archivo Iconografico, S.A./CORBIS; **p41** © Werner Foreman/CORBIS; **p42** (t) © Archivo Iconografico, S.A./CORBIS, (b) © The UCLA Cultural Virtual Reality Laboratory, with thanks to Prof. B. Frischer; **p43** Heritage Images Claudia Severa © The British Museum; **p44** © The ArtArchive; **p45** © The Art Archive; **p46** © Charles & Josette Lenars/CORBIS

Managing designer: Mary Cartwright.
Photographic manipulation: Emma Julings, John Russell, Mike Wheatley.
With thanks to Rachel Firth and Jonathan Sheikh-Miller.

With special thanks to Mike Sigman of Albion Armorers (www.albionarmorers.com) and Chris Haines of the Ermine Street Guard (www.esg.ndirect.co.uk) for their help and advice.